600 Simple Ways to Save on Everything

600 Simple Ways to Save on Everything

John Nardini

Amy Meyering

FAMILY
CHRISTIAN STORES
Helping to Strengthen Hearts, Minds & Souls

600 Simple Ways to Save on Everything by John Nardini and Amy Meyering
Cover and book design by Marty Lenger

Published by Family Christian Stores®

ISBN 1-887654-53-4

Previously published as *600 Simple Tips to Save You Money*

1 2 3 4 5 6 7 8 9 10

Contents

CHRISTIAN STORES

Helping to Strengthen Hearts, Minds & Souls

Dear Valued Guest,

Family Christian Stores has been in the business of impacting lives for Christ for over seventy years. Our company exists to offer a wide selection of Christian products to "help strengthen the hearts, minds and souls" of believers and seekers from all walks of life. This positioning statement is more than just a slogan; it serves as a reminder that above all else, we are a ministry-oriented business.

The book you now hold in your hand is an extension of this mission. The Bible addresses money more than many other topics for good reason. It's a challenge to "store up treasures in heaven" when we live in a society that urges us to keep up with the Joneses. When media bombards us with messages of our supposed need for this or that, it takes supernatural perspective and discipline to remember that we are only managers, not owners, of the resources we possess.

It is our hope that this book will assist you in you stewardship of the assets God has entrusted to you. Filled with great money-saving ideas and valuable coupons, we encourage you to make the most of this helpful guide.

Thank you for shopping Family Christian Stores and Family Christian.com. We appreciate your willingness to allow us to partner with you in reaching our families and communities with the gospel and grace of Jesus Christ. We ask that you pray for us as we seek to operate our company in a way that best fulfills the mission God has given us.

Answering the call to help strengthen the hearts, minds and souls of our guests,

John Nardini
Senior Vice President
Family Christian Stores

The Responsible Use of Credit

By Larry Burkett
Co-founder, Crown Financial Ministries

> *A prudent man sees danger and takes refuge,*
> *but the simple keep going and suffer for it.*
>
> Proverbs 22:3 (NIV)

Credit card debt is a harsh reality for many families. In fact, the average American family carries over seven thousand dollars in credit card debt. But, it is possible—and not at all difficult—for consumers to carry and use credit cards without going into debt. Credit and credit cards do not cause financial problems. It is the abuse and misuse of credit and credit cards that create financial problems. However, through discipline, consumers can enjoy the convenience of credit cards without falling into the debt trap so often associated with the use of credit cards.

Use Your Credit Wisely

The first step to responsible use of a credit card is to understand the difference between credit and debt. Credit involves charging purchases. If you pay your credit cards off completely each month, you are using credit wisely. Debt is incurred when you don't pay the charges off but roll a balance forward month after month. This puts you into debt and can become burdensome.

To avoid debt, always be sure to pay your balance off each month. By doing so, you will never have to pay interest charges. On the same day that you make a charge on your credit card, write a check for the full amount of the purchase and deduct it from your checking account balance. You spent the money, so it is no longer money that is available to spend. As soon as the statement comes in, mail the full payment immediately. If your credit card company charges you a fee for not carrying a balance, cancel the card.

If You Can't Pay

The very first month you have a credit card bill that you cannot pay in full, destroy the credit card, never use it again, do not get another one, and try to pay the balance off as soon as possible. Make the payments as early in the billing month as you can, or make two smaller payments a month if you can't pay early. Most banks calculate interest on the average daily balance. The larger the payment and the sooner in the month you make it, the more of it will apply to the principal.

The following are suggestions on how you can use credit cards for your benefit and convenience and yet not allow them to control you.

- Ask your bank for an extra checkbook register (they generally provide these for free) to keep track of credit card purchases and payments. Do this the same way that you record checking account transactions.

- Remember that every time you charge, you are spending cash. When you charge, write a check to the credit card company right then and there.

- Know the difference between being able to charge it and being able to afford it. Never use credit cards for anything except budgeted purchases.

- Always keep in mind that although you might be able to afford something, that does not mean you have to buy it.

- Carry a credit card with you only if you carry a zero or near-zero balance. If you have a credit card balance, keep the credit cards in a safe, inconvenient place that is out of sight, but do not carry them with you.

- Retain only one all-purpose, no-fee credit card. Cancel all others. Accept a credit limit that you can easily pay in full on your present income, and reject all credit limit increases.

- If stores add a surcharge to your bill for paying with a credit card, you can refuse to pay it. Most credit card companies do not allow vendors to add a surcharge to credit card purchases.

- Never apply for another card when you reach the limit on the one you're using.

Living Debt-Free in a "Charge It!" World

Debt-free living is God's plan for us today. The blessings of becoming debt-free go far beyond the financial arena; they extend to the spiritual realm as well. By following a few simple rules, you can avoid the trap of credit card debt and enjoy spiritual and financial freedom.

For More Information

Crown Financial Ministries provides a range of resources that assist people in understanding God's principles of money management and becoming debt free. You can contact Crown by calling 800-722-1976 or by visiting www.crown.org on the Internet.

Make Your Money Work For You

Banking for the Budget-Minded

The cost of banking has risen in the past several years, but it doesn't have to take a huge bite out of your budget. These simple tips will help you keep more money in your accounts.

1 Join a credit union. Many of these organizations offer low-priced services for their members, including free checking, deals on insurance, financial planning options and great rates on loans.

2 Try Internet banking if it's convenient for you. You can avoid many of the fees brick-and-mortar banks charge.

3 Compare prices on bank services and shop around for a good deal. Request a list of services and fees from several banks to get the best value.

4 Look into discounts. For example, many banks will lower your checking fees if you have your paycheck directly deposited into your account. Ask what other discounts are available.

5 Understand your bank fees. You can avoid many unnecessary charges if you know what the fees are and when you will get penalized.

6 Go into your bank to deposit or withdraw money. You'll get to know the staff (which may come in handy when you apply for a loan or need other services) and avoid costly ATM fees.

7 Balance your checkbook as soon as you receive your statement each month. This allows you to check for errors and avoid expensive fees for bouncing checks or falling below your minimum balance.

8 Order checks from a service other than your financial institution. You can save up to fifty percent on check costs.

9 Avoid getting overdraft protection for your checking account. This service can cause people who are not disciplined about balancing their checkbooks to quickly accumulate debt.

10 Protect the checks you deposit by writing "for deposit only" and your account number on the back. If your checks are lost or stolen before you deposit them, this will ensure they cannot be cashed or deposited into another account.

11 Open a school savings account for your children. These accounts normally don't have service fees or require a minimum balance, plus they're a great way to teach your kids healthy financial concepts from a young age.

What the Bible Says:

But remember the Lord your God, for it is he who gives you the ability to produce wealth, and so confirms his covenant, which he swore to your forefathers, as it is today.

DEUTERONOMY 8:18

Dress For Less

Cutting Your Clothing Costs

Is it possible to keep your wardrobe current without breaking the bank? Absolutely! It's easy to become a savvier shopper, save money and look great. Try these ideas on for size.

Where and How to Shop

12 Assess your clothing needs at the beginning of a season, and make a list of what items you'll need to update or complement your wardrobe. Don't buy more than you need each season.

13 Purchase gently used clothing at consignment shops, thrift stores and yard or rummage sales. This works especially well for maternity and children's clothes, and also for suits, dresses or other higher-end items that can be found at upscale consignment shops. Look carefully for stains or defects in any item. Be sure to try items on to ensure a proper fit—sometimes alterations have been made that affect the size. If you become a regular shopper at one store, get to know the clerks and ask them to call you when new items come in.

14 Shop thrift stores like Goodwill or the Salvation Army for lower-priced clothing. They offer less-expensive items than consignment shops but the quality of clothing is usually not as high. These stores often run specials on items (i.e., clothes are half-price on a certain day of the week). Be sure to call ahead and ask about specials.

15 Save money on kids' clothes by starting a clothing swap with friends, family or a church group.

16 Check out yard or rummage sales for the lowest prices on clothing, especially for infants and children. Shop the garage sales in upscale neighborhoods for good deals on current styles.

17 Take your own clothes to consignment shops and eventually you'll receive checks in the mail for your clothing.

18 Shop end-of-season and clearance sales when you can save anywhere from fifty to seventy-five percent. If you do this at the end of each season, you'll always have new clothes when a season starts!

19 Shop holiday sales like President's Day, Fourth of July and Veterans' Day sales. There are usually some good deals to be found.

20 Check out clearance racks each time you shop. Your persistence will always pay off in great bargains.

21 Inspect clothing thoroughly for holes, stains or other imperfections before you buy. If it's something you have to have, ask for a discount if the item has a flaw.

22 Buy all your children's socks in one color and style so that if one sock from a pair wears out or gets lost, you can just match it up with another.

23 Quickly return any items that don't fit well or you change your mind about. Many stores have a limited time frame in which you can make returns. Educate yourself on the various return policies.

24 Stock your wardrobe with classic pieces that don't quickly go out of style. Buy only one or two trendy items each season, or save more money by using accessories like belts, scarves and ties to stay current instead of purchasing entire outfits.

25 Buy fewer kids' clothes, and wash them more often.

26 Purchase children's clothing on sale, even if the items are too big. You can wait until your kids grow into them or alter them to fit now.

27 Shop the stores at outlet malls for great deals. But buyer beware: sometimes you can get items offered in outlet stores cheaper when they're on sale at the regular store.

28 Try discount retailers like Marshall's®, T.J. Maxx® or Nordstrom Rack® Their inventories continually change, so be persistent and come away with some great bargains.

29 Plan your shopping trips. Don't buy clothes on impulse or you could be passing up a bargain somewhere else.

30 Shop in the men's departments for clothing basics like socks, turtlenecks, etc. They are often cheaper than in women's departments.

31 Shop for clothing labeled as "irregular." The prices are low and the flaws are often not noticeable.

Clothing Care

32 Prevent the heels of your shoes from wearing out by having tips put on the bottom of your shoes.

33 Protect and preserve shoes and leather purses or pocketbooks by spraying them with water/stain repellant.

34 Polish shoes before you wear them for the first time to preserve the leather and protect them from scratches.

35 Resole older shoes and have new lifts put on worn-down heels.

36 Reline your coat—it's often cheaper than buying a new one.

37 Don't throw out a garment because it's missing a button. Replace all of the buttons with new ones.

38 Keep on top of your clothing repair. Fix small tears before they get larger. Sew on loose buttons before they get lost. Treat stains immediately before they set.

39 Remember that a higher price doesn't always mean higher quality. Avoid buying poorly constructed clothes—they simply won't last as long and won't fit as well when you wear them. Look at seams and stitch lengths to help determine the durability of the garment. The stronger the seams, the longer they will last. Check out the fabric to ensure the item won't lose its shape. Make sure that zippers and labels don't pucker.

40 Avoid "dry-clean only" garments. Purchase clothes that can be machine washed to avoid high dry-cleaning bills.

41 Remove and hang up your good clothes as soon as you get home to prevent wrinkles. This will help you save on dry-cleaning.

42 Search out a discount dry-cleaner for your dry-cleaning items. Many charge just $1.50 for any item. Considering that the cost for cleaning a jacket can reach $5.00 or more, that's an incredible savings over time.

43 Wash select delicate items at home to avoid having them dry-cleaned. Be sure to test a seam or inside facing before washing the entire garment.

44 Hand-wash silk blouses and sweaters in cold water with a detergent made for delicate garments.

45 Press men's suits with a damp cloth between the fabric and the iron. Send suits to the dry cleaners just twice a year to preserve the fibers.

46 Spray ties with fabric protector to avoid frequent dry-cleaning.

47 Store your wool sweaters with mothballs during the summer months to help them last longer.

48 Spray the heels and toes of sandalfoot nylons with hairspray to prevent snags and runs.

Stretching Your Wardrobe

49 Coordinate the clothing in your wardrobe with interchangeable pieces. Mix and match pants, jackets, suits, shirts and sweaters in similar color schemes to create multiple outfits from just a few items.

50 Purchase a used tuxedo if you need to wear one frequently. You'll save a fortune on rental fees.

51 Accessorize outfits with scarves, pins or other items. You may be surprised how many different looks you can have with one piece of clothing and several inexpensive accessories.

52 Alter clothes for extended wear instead of getting rid of them. Letting down a hem or letting out some seams can take clothes even further.

53 Use the scrap material from cutting or hemming a garment to make coordinating hair ties, scarves or cloth belts.

54 Take up sewing. You often can sew clothes for about one-third of what they would cost in a store.

55 Rent formal wear if you're a woman. This works especially well for prom dresses and wedding gowns, garments that are usually only worn once.

What the Bible Says:

…When God gives any man wealth and possessions, and enables him to enjoy them, to accept his lot and be happy in his work— this is a gift of God.

ECCLESIASTES 5:19

The Old College Try

Making Higher Education Affordable

When the average college student graduates several thousand dollars in debt, the high cost of higher education can strike fear into the hearts of many parents and students. But there are ways to offset the expense of tuition and lower the amount you have to borrow—or avoid debt altogether.

Before You Go

56 Research the availability of scholarships in your school's counseling office or go online and search through millions of scholarships that offer more than four billion dollars in funding.

57 Take college courses while in high school to reduce the cost of and the time required for a four-year degree. Be sure that these credits will transfer to the school you ultimately hope to attend.

58 Take core classes at a low-cost four-year college or reputable community college before ultimately earning a degree at a more prestigious school.

59 Carefully research the financial aid packages, scholarships and discounts available at the schools you're considering. Make an informed decision about your college funding options.

60 Consider tuition assistance through national service organizations like Americorps. For more information, log onto www.americorps.org.

61 Join a branch of the military to help finance your education. You'll get some great experience and have part or all of your tuition paid.

62 Look into a distance-learning program. Tuition is considerably cheaper and you can often learn at your own pace.

63 Establish residency in the state you'll be attending school to avoid out-of-state tuition costs.

Once You're There

64 Share rides with friends, whether you commute or make it home just a few times each semester.

65 Avoid frequent trips to restaurants. Instead, hit the grocery store and prepare your own meals.

66 Limit the amount you spend on renting videos, DVDs or video games by getting several friends to chip in, or take turns paying the rental fee.

67 Shop for the latest styles at consignment shops or thrift stores instead of the mall. You'll look great without spending a lot.

68 Find an on-campus job. Not only will this fill your time (to avoid "boredom spending") and give you some extra spending money, but it could pad your resume, helping your job prospects in the future.

69 Avoid purchasing soda and other snacks from vending machines. They may be convenient but they can cost you a fortune if you use them frequently.

70 Scout out used furniture (desks, couches, lofts and tables) at the end of the year when people are switching dorm rooms or graduating. You may be able to furnish your own room for free.

71 Take more than the minimum amount of credits you need to retain full-time status. Taking sixteen, seventeen or eighteen credits each semester can reduce the amount of time you're in school (and the amount of money you'll pay).

72 Purchase used textbooks, either from your college bookstore or from students selling their own. This will save you a significant amount of money.

What the Bible Says:

Whoever trusts in his riches will fall, but the righteous will thrive like a green leaf.

PROVERBS 11:28

Leisure Time For Less

Saving While You're At Play

Living on a budget doesn't mean you can't have any fun. In fact, you can find new ways to enjoy yourself and still maintain your financial peace of mind. Look over this list of simple tips and use your imagination to come up with your own.

With the Kids

73 Take advantage of your local parks and play-grounds. Kids love playing on the swings and monkey bars, and you may have the opportunity to meet other parents. Some public parks feature pools or beaches that you can use for free or a small fee.

74 Spend a day together as a family exploring local nature trails, playing at state or county parks or driving to an area beach or lake. Look for ideas at your local Chamber of Commerce.

75 Picnic with your kids in your own backyard. Pack food in their school lunchboxes, spread out a blanket and enjoy your time together.

76 Let your kids run through the sprinkler on a hot day instead of investing in an expensive pool membership for the summer.

77 Create a collage out of colorful autumn leaves pressed between wax paper.

78 Give your kids a section of the garden to plant what they want. Not only will they be kept busy by the work, but it's also a great educational tool.

79 Turn a walk around your neighborhood into a scavenger hunt.

80 Gather old sheets, towels and blankets and watch your kids transform them into a giant tent or fort.

81 Visit museums, zoos, planetariums and aquariums. Many have half-price or free admission days, and some offer unlimited visits with an annual membership. Remember, before investing in an annual membership, take your family at least once to be sure they would be interested in multiple visits.

82 Make a big family dinner. Give everyone a different dish to make or task to complete.

83 Spend an evening gathering items for a donation box to give to a local relief organization or volunteer as a family at a soup kitchen.

84 Assign a week to each member of your family and let that person choose the activities for every day.

85 Make homemade birdfeeders using pine cones and peanut butter. Use the project to teach your kids about the different kinds of birds native to your area.

86 Buy board games at a local thrift store (they're usually two dollars or less) and spend time together as a family playing them.

87 Look into a YMCA membership for your family. You can swim, lift weights, participate in exercise classes, ice skate, roller skate and much more each day of the week for a nominal monthly fee.

88 Find books at the library outlining fun activities like making kites, cooking or puppet shows and do them together as a family.

89 Go on a factory tour. Many companies offer free tours of their facilities that are entertaining and educational.

90 Let your kids make edible necklaces out of cereal or macaroni. You can purchase the generic or off-brand varieties of colorful cereal or pasta and watch your kids get creative.

91 Help your kids write and illustrate their own auto-biographies. Not only is this a unique way to capture a family history, but these projects will become cherished possessions.

Dating on a Budget

92 Make some homemade cappuccino or hot choco-late, head to a park and watch the sun set.

93 Explore an area nature or walking trail.

94 Picnic anywhere—the beach, a park or your living room floor!

95 Dress up in your very best and slow dance to your favorite love songs, all in the comfort of your own home.

96 Spend an evening test-driving your favorite cars.

97 Take your time strolling through a free art gallery or museum.

98 Get together with friends or neighbors and start a babysitting co-op to avoid spending money on childcare. They can take the kids for a few hours while you and your spouse enjoy your date, and you can return the favor when it's their turn.

99 Spend some time browsing through your favorite bookstore. It's a quiet, peaceful place, and you can even catch up on some of your reading.

100 Go out for breakfast instead of dinner—it's significantly cheaper.

101 Enjoy a picnic in your car. Pack food and park in an out-of-the-way area, a local park, scenic overlook or airport observation point. Bring along your favorite cassettes or CDs and spend time talking and getting to know each other.

102 Take a drive in the evening to give yourselves time away from the phone, TV and household chores. This works especially well for parents of young children—you can talk while they sleep in the back seat.

103 Go on an "educational date." Attend a class or read a book and discuss it together. Take in a lecture at a museum.

104 Take in free rehearsals. Many theater groups, ballet companies and symphonies open rehearsals to the public for free.

105 Spend an evening looking through your wedding album or other family pictures. It's a great way to reconnect and share special memories.

Entertainment

106 Cancel your cable. How often do you flip through the channels and find nothing that piques your interest? Turn off the TV and spend some quality time with family or friends.

107 Save money on movies by renting videos or DVDs. Many video stores offer specials on their selections. Better yet, check out the rentals at your local library. They're often cheaper or even free.

108 Get active by doing things that get you outside and exercising like biking, hiking, in-line skating or tossing a Frisbee.

109 Take advantage of the activities at the college or university in your community. They offer everything from art shows and poetry readings to movies and sporting events.

110 Spend time at community events that often go unnoticed: Little League games, bingo nights, pancake breakfasts, Special Olympics and fundraisers.

111 Attend musicals and plays at local high schools, community colleges and universities. It's entertaining and you'll be giving to a good cause.

112 Check the event section of your local newspaper for free concerts, festivals and events. Many cities offer great entertainment like this, especially during the summer months.

113 Take advantage of low-priced matinees or special discounts at movie theaters. Bring in your own snacks. Ask if your employer, bank or credit union sells half-price tickets to movies.

114 Host a potluck dinner. Pick a theme, invite friends and enjoy good food and great company.

What the Bible Says:

The blessing of the Lord brings wealth, and he adds no trouble to it.

PROVERBS 10:22

Family Food Savings

Financially Feasible Shopping and Cooking

Food can take a major bite out of your budget, especially when you take a look at the amount you spend at the grocery store and fast food drive-thru. By following these simple ideas, you'll spend less and get more at the store, in the kitchen and at your favorite restaurant.

Save With Coupons

115 Subscribe to an online coupon newsletter and get notified of all the great new discount codes and bargains each day.

116 Be wise about your coupon clipping. Don't purchase something just because you have a coupon for it. Be sure you're getting the best value for the products you need.

117 Start a coupon swap with friends and neighbors and trade the coupons you don't need for ones you can use. Some grocery stores offer coupon bins that allow customers to swap coupons.

118 Subscribe to coupon-related magazines and news-papers.

119 Call into a company's consumer line or send comments via its website. They often give coupons and special offers to those who do.

120 Research a store's coupon policy. Does it offer double or triple coupon days? Does it produce its own coupons? How can you get them?

121 Categorize your coupons so you can access them more easily. Use a recipe box or envelopes. Be sure to go through them every so often and throw out the ones that have expired.

122 Go through stores' promotional ads each week and match your coupons to the specials. Make your grocery list based on what you find.

123 Use both a manufacturer and store coupon on the same one-item purchase. Be sure to check any disclaimers that would not allow this.

124 Ask the store where you buy your Sunday paper if you can have the extra coupon sections after they've sold all the newspapers they're going to sell for the day.

125 Use coupons on sale items. Instead of using them the week you clip them out, hold on to your coupons and save them for sale items.

Grocery Shopping

126 Go through the items in your kitchen before you shop to avoid multiple trips to the store. Make your list based on what you need, the weekly specials and the coupons you have. Be sure to indicate which items you have a coupon for so you don't forget to use it. Plan your weekly menu around what is on sale.

127 Use clothespins to keep food tightly sealed. It will stay fresher for a longer period of time.

128 Make the discount bin at the grocery store a stop each time you're there. You can save a lot of money on slightly damaged packages.

129 Avoid buying convenience foods like TV dinners, frozen pizza, etc.

130 Buy household staples like paper towels, toilet paper, pasta, flour and sugar in bulk and split them with a friend.

131 Have a plan of action when you grocery shop and get only the items on your list. Studies show that shoppers spend an extra fifty cents for every minute over thirty they spend in the store.

132 Buy off-brand or generic products instead of brand names. You're often getting the same quality but at a lower price.

133 Get the most out of your meat purchases: Learn to quarter a whole chicken or purchase chicken with the skin still on it. Skinless chicken is often more expensive. Be sure to compare costs by the pound.

134 Ask for a rain check when a sale item is out of stock.

135 Stock up when you find a great deal. Try to buy at least a month's worth of the product.

136 Remember that cheese in the dairy case is often cheaper than the cheese available in the deli.

137 Buy fruits and vegetables in season.

138 Carefully watch the price scanner when your purchases are rung up, and double-check your receipt before you leave the store.

139 Purchase unsweetened drink mix instead of soft drinks. Not only will you save money, but also you can limit your family's sugar intake.

140 Avoid grocery shopping when you're hungry. If you shop on an empty stomach you'll usually end up buying more than you planned on.

141 Compare the unit prices of similar items to get the best deal possible.

142 Keep an eye on sale prices and advertised specials to ensure that you really are getting the best value. Sometimes you'll find that what appears to be a good deal really isn't.

143 Take advantage of programs that offer nearly-free items if you send proofs of purchase.

144 Buy the less expensive white eggs instead of brown.

145 Ask the attendants in the fish, bakery and deli departments to make you a deal on their prices. This works especially well in the evenings when they are looking to sell through their stock for the day.

146 Purchase non-food items like detergent, shampoo, garbage bags and toothpaste at a discount pharmacy or larger discount retailer like Wal-Mart or Target. These items are often more expensive at grocery stores.

147 Compare the weight and prices of similar items that have different packaging. It's generally believed that items packaged in bags are less expensive, but this isn't always the case. Take your time and do your homework.

148 Keep track of the prices of items you would like to purchase. This will help you recognize a good deal when it comes around.

149 Look into a membership at a co-op or buying club. Purchasing food directly from wholesalers can save you up to fifty percent.

150 Shop around and compare prices at area grocery stores. Use their customer loyalty programs to save yourself money.

151 Search out an area butcher to get the best prices on meat.

152 Purchase fruits and vegetables from roadside stands or farmers' markets. Not only are their prices lower, but they may also be open to negotiating a cheaper price.

153 Find creative, but ethical, solutions to bypass limits on sale items by having each member in your family purchase the number allowed.

154 Learn what days your local grocery store runs specials on day-old bread, marks down damaged packages, etc. Plan your shopping accordingly.

155 Purchase whole or half hams and turkey breasts and have the grocery store deli slice it thinly for you. This is much less expensive than buying packaged deli meats.

156 Purchase a freezer and use it to stock up on items when they're on sale.

157 Set limits on how much you'll be willing to pay for food items at the grocery store and stick to them. This will help you avoid overspending.

158 Find the loss leaders at your grocery store. These items are sold at or just below cost to draw you into the store in hopes that you'll buy more.

Meal Preparation

159 Prepare meals ahead of time and freeze them. When you're crunched for time, you simply have to pull a meal out of the freezer, avoiding the cost of hitting a drive-thru or ordering a pizza.

160 Purchase a baby food grinder (about seven dollars) and save on baby food. It grinds most foods to a consistency safe for infants to eat, and you can prepare the same meal for everyone in your family.

161 Always have the ingredients for several quick and simple meals on hand to throw something together in a pinch.

162 Get creative with your meal preparation. Make new dishes with the ingredients you have on hand.

163 Help your flavored gourmet coffee go further by combining it with regular coffee. Simply mix together equal parts of each and you'll get twice as many pots of gourmet per pound.

164 Make your own salad dressings. They are quick, simple and inexpensive to prepare.

165 Take a break from grocery shopping and use up the surplus food you have in your cupboards and refrigerator.

166 Make your own breadcrumbs and croutons.

167 Bring your lunch to work or school instead of eating out. You can fill a thermos with soup, coffee or tea and keep your favorite liquids warm. Fill small containers with applesauce or pudding instead of purchasing more expensive individual servings.

168 Make your own "snack packs" by filling store brand sandwich bags with chips, cookies, pretzels or other snacks. Put together ten at a time and you'll have them on hand to include in lunches or available anytime someone has the munchies. You can even reuse the bags—just rinse them out and let them dry.

169 Plant your own vegetable and herb garden.

170 Save on your meat purchases by preparing vegetarian meals every so often.

171 Bring your own snacks to work instead of making daily trips to the vending machine.

172 Be sure to use up all of the items in your freezer. Have leftover night, or experiment with the ingredients you have on hand. This will save you money and give you a chance to clean out and defrost the freezer.

173 Fill your freezer with frozen treats that you've made to avoid expensive trips to the ice cream truck during the summer.

174 Cook and bake from scratch as often as you can. It's less expensive than eating out or buying a ready-to-eat meal or mix, plus it's often more nutritious.

175 Make your own snacks like popcorn (learn to pop it on the stove instead of the microwave), trail mix, frozen grapes, etc.

176 Make the most of your food dollar by using everything. Use meat bones and vegetable trimmings for soup stock. Leftover meats and vegetables can be used in stews, soups, pot pies and casseroles.

177 Purchase a bread machine. Prices have come down in recent years, and it can be much more economical to bake your own bread instead of purchasing it at the store each week.

178 Learn to can your own fruits and vegetables. It may take a little extra time, but the convenience and low cost are worth it.

Dining Out

179 Visit restaurants only when they offer two-for-one deals or other promotional specials.

180 Dine out for breakfast or lunch. Prices are typically lower than during the dinner hour.

181 Order the special of the day. It's a good value.

182 Take advantage of the free birthday meals offered at local restaurants. It's a fun and inexpensive way to celebrate your special day.

183 Plan to eat out during the week instead of the weekend when prices tend to be higher.

184 Share an entrée or order an appetizer if you don't have a large appetite.

185 Avoid purchasing desserts since their prices are usually high. If you'd really like to have one, share it with your dining partner.

186 Use frequent dining cards or purchase a coupon book for restaurants in your area.

187 Write off any meals you eat out for business purposes if you own a business. Consult your accountant for the percentage allowed.

188 Dine at all-you-can-eat buffet restaurants, especially if you have a family.

189 Thoroughly check your bill for errors, either in your favor or against you. Either way, kindly point out any errors and your honesty may be rewarded.

190 Drink water instead of ordering soda or other drinks when eating out.

What the Bible Says:

Keep your lives free from the love of money and be content with what you have, because God has said, "Never will I leave you, never will I forsake you."

HEBREWS 13:5

Simple And Sweet
Gift Giving for Any Occasion

L ooking for unique gift ideas for Christmas, birthdays or other special occasions that won't break the bank? There are hundreds of fun and inexpensive ways to show someone you care. Here's a sampling.

Simple Gift Ideas

191 Write and frame a letter that lets the recipient know how much he or she means to you.

192 Give a set of wind chimes as a housewarming gift. They are relatively inexpensive and add a unique touch to any home.

193 Make chocolate covered pretzels, spiced tea mix or other easy-to-prepare food items and package them in attractive gift containers.

194 Make a unique care package for those new to the area. Highlight areas of interest on a street map like parks, bike trails, restaurants, zoos and museums. Add a list of reliable service technicians, doctors, dentists and pharmacies.

195 Create unique note cards by pressing flowers and gluing them to a heavier weight paper.

196 Give an IOU coupon book to a friend or family member. They can "redeem" their coupons for things like free babysitting, a cup of coffee, a car wash, house cleaning, etc.

197 Write down simple recipes and collect them in a recipe box for a recent college graduate or newlywed couple.

198 Give inexpensive and simple games like checkers, dominoes and Yahtzee®.

199 Give a disposable camera, along with a coupon for film developing, as a gift for any age.

200 Put together a stationery set. Include envelopes, special occasion cards, writing pads and stamps.

201 Take the time to make homemade cards. They are less expensive and much more meaningful.

202 Share the flowers in your garden. Purchase an empty vase and attach a note that offers the recipient a chance to gather blooms from your garden.

203 Fill a large bucket or waste basket with cleaning supplies for someone moving into their first home or apartment.

204 Make your own tasty treat for chilly evenings by dipping plastic spoons (purchase ones in festive colors) into melted chocolate, shaking off the excess and placing them on wax paper to harden. You can sprinkle crushed peppermint candies over the chocolate before it hardens as an added treat. Wrap the spoons in cellophane, tie a ribbon and place several in a mug along with hot chocolate packets.

205 Make your own gift basket of bath salts (which you can easily make yourself), a scented candle and a cassette or CD of relaxing music.

206 Give grandparents family or school pictures already framed.

207 Make homemade vinegars, spice mixes and mustards. Your local library will have cookbooks with recipes for these unique gifts.

208 Give a plant started from the clippings of a plant like ivy. This makes a great housewarming gift when given in an attractive tin or flowerpot.

209 Send cards for birthdays instead of gifts.

210 Make an audio or video recording of your family for friends and relatives who live out of state.

Christmas/Holidays

211 Personalize holiday ornaments with a brief message and the date.

212 Spend time with just your immediate family during the Christmas season to cut down on travel expenses.

213 Purchase gifts only for immediate family members.

214 Begin a gift exchange with members of your extended family so you won't have to buy gifts for every person.

215 Send gift certificates instead of gifts. You'll save on shipping, and you'll be sure to give a gift the recipient wants.

216 Make gifts for grandparents with your kids. Both the giver and the recipient will have a wonderful time with each other and the gift.

217 Make your own wrapping paper using butcher's paper, along with crayons, markers, glitter, rubber-stamps or paint. The kids will love helping out with this task!

218 Send Christmas postcards instead of regular cards to save on postage. You can even get creative and cut the front half from last year's Christmas cards to use as postcards.

219 Shop the after-Christmas sales for wrapping paper, cards, ornaments and other holiday items. You'll be able to save fifty percent to seventy-five percent.

220 Take in a holiday parade with your family. Bring along your own hot chocolate and snacks.

221 Attend free local holiday celebrations like tree trimmings, concerts and carol singing. Invite friends and neighbors to go with you—the more, the merrier!

222 Tour neighborhoods to see Christmas lights. Many have contests for the most unique, most traditional, etc., so you're bound to see some great displays.

223 Make it a family project to learn all you can about a certain holiday, or how that holiday is celebrated in different countries. Discuss what you've learned and try implementing some new traditions into your own celebrations.

Parties

224 Purchase brightly colored plates, cups, napkins and table coverings at a dollar store or half-off card shop.

225 Create your own party themes. Get imaginative with food, games and party favors and save money.

226 Do your own baking and cooking instead of purchasing ready-made items from the store.

227 Pick up inexpensive trinkets throughout the year to include in goodie bags at birthday parties.

228 Search for affordable at-home entertainment. You may find someone who moonlights as a magician or clown at an inexpensive rate.

229 Plan your party for a weekday instead of a weekend. Many places that host kids' parties charge more on Fridays and Saturdays.

What the Bible Says:

Humility and fear of the Lord bring wealth and honor and life.

PROVERBS 22:4

Tithes And Offerings

Understanding the Importance of Giving

Give privately and prayerfully. Then it can be done with the proper spirit—joyfully—as we thank God for His provision and the privilege of helping others in need. Here are some ideas for incorporating regular giving into your financial plans in order to make a difference.

230 Study what the Bible says about giving. Read books on giving from Christian financial experts (see the listing of resources at the end of this book). Ask your pastor for additional resources.

231 Make giving a priority. Always set aside a percentage of your budget (many Christian financial planners recommend ten percent) to give to your church or another organization important to you.

232 Keep it simple. If you're just beginning, take a look at your budget and determine what percentage you can give. Gradually increase that percentage over time.

233 Give from the extra money you receive throughout the year, like tax refunds, bonuses, raises or even money raised from a garage sale.

234 Get creative. Donate clothes, an unneeded car, stocks or free services from your business. Collect spare change and give it away at the end of the month.

235 Volunteer your time and talents to a ministry or service organization.

236 Adopt a family in need. Check with your church or another ministry organization and help a family out with odd jobs, babysitting, buying groceries, etc.

What the Bible Says:

Honor the Lord with your wealth, with the first fruits of all your crops; then your barns will be filled to overflowing, and your vats will brim over with new wine.

PROVERBS 3:9-10

Healthy Living For A Healthy Budget

Saving on Insurance and Medical Costs

The cost of health care has skyrocketed in recent years and the maze of insurance, doctor networks and medical procedures can be difficult to navigate financially. Here are some ideas for keeping these costs under control.

Please Note: These tips are for informational purposes only and should not be construed as medical advice. All medical decisions/questions should be referred to your health care professional and discussed in the context of your individual needs and problems.

Preventive Care

237 Exercise on a regular basis. Not only will you look and feel better, but it's also a great way to prevent a host of medical conditions.

238 Play with your kids. Get outside and throw a baseball, toss a Frisbee or shoot hoops.

239 Eat sensibly. Make meals from scratch and eat fruits, vegetables and grains. You'll save money and eat healthy at the same time.

240 Keep up on your annual physical exams and immunizations. This is the best way to prevent small problems from becoming bigger ones.

241 Quit smoking. Not only will you avoid a long list of health problems, but you'll also save quite a bit of money.

242 Keep your weight under control to avoid future health problems and costly trips to weight loss clinics.

243 Brush and floss at least once a day to avoid large dental bills.

244 Utilize government-sponsored immunizations, especially for your children. These services are available at a low cost, or even free.

Prescription Drugs

245 Check into payment assistance programs for prescription drugs. Many low-income individuals and families qualify for some sort of assistance. Ask your doctor or pharmacist.

246 Purchase generic over-the-counter and prescription drugs. Ask your doctor for recommendations or alternatives when he or she prescribes medicine.

247 Compare drug prices at local pharmacies. Be sure you have the drug name, dosage and quantity on hand when you call or stop by.

248 Look into mail-order services from organizations like AARP, Good SAM Travel Club or MedExpress for on-going prescriptions. This will save you both time and money.

Other Healthy Tips

249 Examine your benefit plan carefully. Know what is covered and what is not so you don't end up with expensive surprises.

250 Check to see if your employer offers a Flex spending plan. This is a great way to supplement your insurance coverage.

251 Carefully look over your doctor bills and insurance statements to ensure everything is correct.

252 Get a second opinion before undergoing an extensive medical procedure. This may help you avoid paying a large deductible.

253 See what services a local dental or medical school has to offer. You may be able to get free or low-cost exams.

254 Look into the other health plans offered by your employer. You want to be sure you're getting the best value.

255 Ask for an itemized bill for your hospital stay. The majority of hospital bills contain errors, so it definitely pays to get and carefully study an itemized bill.

256 Seek out a group you can join to receive group medical coverage. This form of insurance usually offers the most benefits for the lowest coverage. Check with a credit union or local civic club.

Life Insurance

257 Buy a term life insurance policy if you're in need of insurance protection only and not looking for a long-term investment.

258 Hold a whole life, universal life or other cash value policy for at least fifteen years. Canceling earlier than that may double your life insurance costs.

Funeral Spending

259 Put your wishes regarding your funeral, memorial or burial arrangements in writing. This will save you and your family money and additional worry.

260 Do your research before choosing a funeral home. Call several and ask about their prices for specific services, or stop by and get an itemized price list.

261 Get in touch with a local memorial society (find them in the Yellow Pages under "funeral services"). They can advise you of the least costly options for funeral arrangements and save you thousands of dollars.

262 Be cautious about pre-paying for your funeral. There may be risks and additional costs involved.

What the Bible Says:

Be sure to know the condition of your flocks, give careful attention to your herds; for riches do not endure forever, and a crown is not secure for all generations.

PROVERBS 27:23-24

Home Sweet Home

The Dollars and Cents of Home Ownership and Renting

While a home is one of the best investments you can make, it can also be costly. It pays to do your research and make informed decisions about your housing costs. Here are some ways to do just that.

Mortgages

263 Refinance your mortgage. With today's low interest rates, refinancing your mortgage could save you thousands of dollars. By lowering your rate only 1.5%, you'll save more than $64 a month over fifteen years on a $75,000 mortgage (a total savings of almost $11,600). Many banks will forego the closing costs as a way to thank you for your patronage.

264 Pre-pay your mortgage. Even just a few dollars extra every week will save you a significant amount on interest over the life of the mortgage.

265 Do your research and get the shortest-term mortgage you can afford. For example, you will pay $90,000 less in interest on a fifteen-year mortgage than on a thirty-year mortgage with $100,000 fixed-rate loan at eight percent annual percentage rate. Plus, find the lowest rate with the lowest points. Taking the same example, lowering the APR from 8.5% to 8.0% can save you over $5,000 in interest and paying two points instead of three could save an additional $1,000.

266 Cancel Private Mortgage Insurance (PMI) after you own twenty percent of your home.

267 Research other mortgage options, such as FHA (Federal Housing Administration), Veteran's Administration or other government-sponsored loan programs.

Buying and Selling a Home

268 Make sure your loan is pre-approved so that you know exactly how much money you'll be working with.

269 Check out a home's construction quality before you purchase. Look at the plumbing, roof, foundation, windows and overall structure to avoid costly repairs in the future.

270 Get estimates on the work you'll need to do on a fixer-upper. Don't bite off more than you can chew.

271 Negotiate rates with your lawyer when purchasing a home. Watch for any services that could be duplicated by the bank's lawyer.

272 Find a buyer broker who works for you, not the seller, when purchasing a home. This person can often negotiate a better deal for you.

273 Use an inspector of your choice when buying a home. Don't go ahead with the purchase until the house has been properly inspected.

274 Purchase a home around the holidays, if possible. Sales generally fall during this time of year, which gives you greater negotiating power.

275 Negotiate your closing costs, like document preparation fees, loan fees and attorney costs.

276 Make your house as attractive as possible when selling. Make repairs, keep the lawn mowed, plant some flowers and thoroughly clean your home.

277 Sell your home yourself if that option works for you. Be sure to educate yourself beforehand and in the end, you'll save on realtor fees and other costs.

278 Purchase the home you can afford. Experts recommend that your total housing costs (including mortgage payments, taxes, utilities and insurance) not exceed thirty-eight percent of your net income.

279 Consider adding a replacement-cost rider to your renter's or homeowner's insurance. This can cost a little more up front but will save you a significant amount of money if you have a claim because, without this rider, your insurance company will depreciate the value of each item.

280 Ask if the lender servicing your mortgage provides an interest rate reduction if payments are automatically deducted from your checking account.

Renting

281 Choose to rent if you plan to live in an area three years or less. The costs of buying and selling in that short amount of time probably will cancel out any profits on price appreciation.

282 Look beyond classified ads and referrals when searching out an apartment or other rental property. Find a place that you like and ask the owner or building manager if anything is available.

283 Use your skills and talents. Ask your landlord if you can help out around your complex or other rental properties in exchange for taking some money off your rent.

284 Rent out unused rooms in your home to a college student or single person. Rent unused space as storage.

285 Find a roommate. If you're single, a roommate can help ease the burden of rent, food and utilities.

286 Read the fine print when you sign your lease agreement, especially when renting a house. Your signature most likely requires you to make all monthly payments for the life of the lease.

Insurance

287 Ask your insurance agent or broker about discounts. Some companies offer them for non-smokers, retirees, if you have another policy with them or if you have certain safety devices like a monitored security system, deadbolts and fire extinguishers.

288 Shop around for homeowner's and renter's insurance. Call a minimum of five insurance agencies for quotes.

289 Increase the amount of your deductible. Two hundred dollars is usually standard, but raising it to five hundred or one thousand dollars can reduce your overall cost by about seventy-five dollars each year.

Other Tips

290 Evaluate your home. If you have more than enough space, you may want to consider down-sizing to a smaller house or condominium.

291 Compare your property tax assessment with your neighbors' to ensure you are paying the right amount. These records are available at the assessor's office.

292 Do your homework when it comes to contractors. Make sure they are licensed and reputable. Look over their written, fixed-price bids carefully and do not sign a contract that requires full payment up front. Ask them to guarantee their work in writing.

293 Compare prices when looking for a home equity loan. See what at least four banks can offer you when it comes to the APR, points, closing costs and fees.

294 Learn to do simple home repairs instead of calling a service technician each time something goes wrong. You can take a class or check out the home repair guides at your library.

295 Keep up on home maintenance and reduce the risk of damage and injury. Have your furnace serviced regularly, keep your chimney clean, check your roof and turn off the outside water during the winter.

What the Bible Says:

Do not store up for yourselves treasures on earth, where moth and rust destroy, and where thieves break in and steal. But store up for yourselves treasures in heaven, where moth and rust do not destroy, and where thieves do not break in and steal. For where your treasure is, there your heart will be also.

MATTHEW 6:19-21

Creative Kid Spending

Buying on a Budget for Babies and Kids

Raising kids today doesn't have to be expensive. In fact, there are a number of ways you can save money on toys, clothes and other necessities without going outside the limits of your budget. Here's how.

Play Time for Kids

296 Make your own play dough. Simply mix one-quarter cup salt, one-half cup flour and one teaspoon cream of tarter in a saucepan. Add one-half cup water, one-half teaspoon cooking oil and several drops of food coloring. Cook the mixture over medium heat, stirring constantly for one to two minutes until it's the right consistency. Kids have a great time playing with it and it lasts for a long time when stored in locking plastic bags.

297 Encourage your children's creativity by letting them play with household items like Tupperware®, pots and pans or large boxes. You never know where their imagination might take them!

298 Make puppets from wooden spoons. Kids will have fun painting on a face, gluing on yarn for hair and making clothing.

299 Use a large hamper or wicker trunk as a toy box now and storage for other items in the future.

300 Shop garage sales in higher-income neighborhoods. You may be able to find great deals on name-brand clothes and toys.

301 Make a kid-sized table by sawing down the legs on a regular size table.

Babies

302 Surf the Internet for deals on baby items like diapers and formula. You can sign up on mailing lists at manufacturers' websites and receive coupons, special offers and samples.

303 Purchase canned formula instead of the pre-measured packets. It's less expensive and allows you to prepare as much or as little as you need.

304 Check at consignment shops for formula. Many people decide to consign their unused formula after their children have outgrown it.

305 Use cloth diapers instead of disposables. They are less expensive to purchase and can be washed and reused. Purchase inexpensive washcloths for diaper wipes which can be washed and reused.

306 Breastfeed your baby if you are able. It's cheaper and much better for your child than formula.

307 Think economically about the baby products you need. For example, regular towels work just as well as hooded towels, and diapers can be stored anywhere, not just in a specially designed diaper holder.

308 Purchase used furniture and refinish it in the colors that will match your child's bedroom.

309 Fashion bibs out of old towels or sweatshirts.

310 Do your homework before making purchases for baby items like strollers, car seats, high chairs, etc. Ask your relatives, friends and neighbors what they recommend. Also, many websites have places for parents to post their comments on certain products.

311 Decorate your kids' rooms with classic colors and styles that will last them through their teenage years. There aren't too many fifteen-year-olds who will want a "Blue's Clues" bedroom.

312 Make your own booster seat by wrapping two or three old phone books with duct tape. If you'd like, you can cover it with fabric to make it more attractive.

Other Tips

313 Look into scholarships or ask for a hardship discount if your children attend private schools. You may also be able to get a tuition discount if you volunteer regularly at school.

314 Consider home schooling. While this may not be a suitable option for every family, it can be a great way for your kids to get a hands-on education and save you money.

315 Find out about the day camps available in your area during the summer. It's a great way for your kids to have fun without the high cost of sending them to an expensive overnight camp.

316 Encourage your child to get a paper route and make it a family affair. You can use this time to teach him about the principles of money management, and he'll earn his own money instead of getting an allowance from you.

What the Bible Says:

I was young and now I am old, yet I have never seen the righteous forsaken or their children begging bread. They are always generous and lend freely; their children will be blessed.

PSALM 37:25-26

Cents-ible Spending

Creating Budgets and Sticking to Them

One of the easiest ways to save money is to simply reduce your spending. You'll be surprised how many ways there are to cut costs and increase your cash flow.

The Basics

317 Track your cash spending for thirty days. You may be surprised by what you discover about your spending habits. After you track these expenditures, determine what you can spend and what you can save.

318 Develop a budget and stick to it. It may be difficult at first, but when you follow it, you will have financial freedom and peace of mind.

319 Limit your ATM withdrawls. You'll avoid expensive fees and be able to stick to your budget better.

320 Set aside three to six months of living expenses in an emergency fund. This will cover unexpected car repair, medical expenses or job losses. It may be tempting, but don't touch this money unless a true emergency arises.

321 Keep your financial records organized and updated. File checks, bank statements, tax returns and other financial documents in such a way that they are easy to find and access.

322 Take the time to study money management and other financial principles. You'll be educated, informed and have a brighter financial outlook.

323 Transfer credit card balances from your high-interest cards to lower-interest cards.

324 Consult a professional if you have any questions. You want to avoid mistakes on your taxes, will, retirement plan, etc.

325 Spend some time with friends trading saving and spending secrets. Not only will you enjoy fun and fellowship, but you'll also come away with innovative ways to save money.

326 Limit the amount of cash you carry to avoid impulse spending.

Household Spending

327 Keep up on routine maintenance for your household appliances, cars and home. They will run more efficiently and last longer.

328 Use newspapers as an alternative to the more expensive mulch available at nurseries and garden supply stores. Layering newspaper underneath your existing mulch will help stop weed growth and promote moisture retention. Since it's biodegradable, the newspaper will turn into soil.

329 Do your own yard work and landscaping.

330 Save in your garden by planting perennials or self-seeding annuals. They may cost more initially but will bloom year after year.

331 Begin all your plants from seed to make gardening less expensive. Swap seeds with friends and neighbors.

332 Plant flowers, trees and bushes in the fall. They're less expensive that time of year, and more garden experts are now recommending it for better plant health.

333 Purchase concentrated cleaners in bulk from a local janitorial supply company. They are often less expensive and will last longer than many household cleaners found in stores.

334 Ask for samples at department store cosmetic counters.

335 Purchase furniture that requires assembly. It's less expensive and generally easy to put together.

336 Hold off on buying a new computer until you are sure you need one. Take advantage of hardware and software upgrades in the meantime.

337 Research the cost of a pet before you get one. It's amazing how quickly food, vet visits, grooming, boarding and the extra cleaning can add up.

338 Get your hair cut at a beauty school. Their services are significantly cheaper than salon prices.

339 Use woodstove pellets as cat liter. Available at your local feed and grain or hardware store, these pellets are non-clumping, smell great and are much less expensive than regular cat litter.

340 Look at the furniture available at scratch-and-dent stores or the clearance centers of retail furniture and appliance stores. Be sure to check out the items thoroughly because many are sold as-is.

341 Dry one load right after another. The dryer will already be warm from the first load and the second will dry more quickly.

342 Buy white towels instead of colored ones. You can wash them with regular bleach instead of more expensive detergents designed to protect against discoloration and fading.

343 Ask your contractor if you can do part of the job and receive a reduced rate on the total fee.

344 Use the right amount of toothpaste and make it last longer. A pea-sized drop or a thin layer covering the bristles is enough.

345 Get a free e-mail account through services like Yahoo or Microsoft Hotmail and search out a low-cost Internet Service Provider (ISP).

346 Power wash your house instead of investing in a new paint job. Sometimes, that's all it needs.

347 Load your own belongings when making a move. In fact, you can save up to fifty percent on an interstate move if you load things yourself and leave the driving to someone else.

348 Use a camcorder to make a video of your valuables. In the event of something catastrophic, this video will come in handy when making an insurance claim.

349 Consider taking the bus to work if you live in an area where this is convenient for you. This can help you avoid expensive gas and parking costs.

350 Hire a painter during the late fall or winter months. Their services are in higher demand during the summer, leading to higher prices, while their rates are often cheaper in the off-season.

Shopping

351 Develop a resistance to sales pressure and tactics. The easiest way to stick to your budget is to live within your means.

352 Learn the difference between needing something and wanting it when you shop. Too often, we purchase things we want but don't necessarily need, which can lead to more spending than we can afford.

353 Use the Internet to comparison shop and make informed decisions about large purchases. One helpful site is www.MySimon.com, which was rated Forbes' Favorite in Comparison Shopping by *Forbes* magazine.

354 Visit the mall only when you have a specific purchase to make. Window shopping or browsing can lead to impulse buying.

355 Pay for large ticket items in cash. Not only will you avoid incurring unnecessary debt by spending outside of your budget, but you may also get a discount for making a purchase this way.

356 Look into the rebate programs available at drug stores. Many items will end up being free after a rebate.

357 Make major purchases at the end of the month or quarter. This is when retailers and suppliers have to meet their quotas so they will be more open to negotiation.

358 Shop estate sales and auctions. You can often find furniture and other household items in great condition.

359 Buy Christmas presents, birthday gifts and other items off-season. You can save quite a bit of money by shopping sales and clearance racks.

360 Set up a limited weekly allowance for small items like candy bars, soda, gum and other treats. You'll be amazed how much you spend when you add all this up.

361 Avoid impulse buying. Tell yourself to wait at least two days before purchasing something you really want. Usually, the desire will be gone after that amount of time has passed.

362 Bargain for lower prices. You may be surprised how open retailers are to your suggestions.

363 Barter and trade instead of paying cash. Offer to exchange a skill you have or product you make for music lessons, yard work, plumbing or electrical service, car repair, etc.

364 Ask for a discount if an item is slightly flawed.

365 Purchase a display model. They are often priced less or you can negotiate a discount.

366 Watch for seasonal sales. For example, bedding and towels are usually on sale during January, May and August. Learn the patterns, plan in advance and save!

367 Shop according to the weather. If it's a cool, wet summer, you may be able to find a good deal on a swimming pool. If you have a warm winter, snow blowers will probably be marked down.

368 Take advantage of price-matching policies at retailers and use them when you make large purchases.

369 Check into the shipping charges when ordering items through mail-order catalogs. You may find a good deal on an item but end up paying a fortune in shipping.

370 Stick to your guns when dealing with a salespeople. Don't allow them to control the conversation and negotiation, and don't let them talk you into any extras that will up the selling price.

371 Purchase last year's model, especially when buying cars and appliances.

372 Don't purchase a service contract when buying an appliance. Instead, set aside a little more each month in a "repair fund" and be prepared.

373 Shop at furniture outlets in North Carolina, where many furniture items are manufactured. You can often save fifty to eighty percent off of the retail price.

What the Bible Says:

No servant can serve two masters. Either he will hate the one and love the other, or he will be devoted to the one and despise the other. You cannot serve both God and Money.

LUKE 16:3

Don't Dread April 15

Saving on Your Tax Return

Income taxes don't have to be a source of financial frustration each year. If you have a good understanding of tax basics, you can end up ahead instead of paying needlessly. Get started with these easy-to-follow tips.

374 Take advantage of retirement plan incentives. You can lower your taxable income by a substantial amount when you make the maximum contribution to your IRA, 401(k), 403(b), 457 or Keogh plans. Plus, those tax-deferred earnings grow until you retire.

375 Choose the most advantageous filing status. Many taxpayers unwittingly overpay because they don't know whether to file jointly or separately. If you're unsure, consult an accountant or professional tax preparer for advice.

376 Itemize your return. Itemizing requires careful record keeping, but it can reduce your tax liability considerably.

377 Adjust your withholding to reflect your income so you won't pay too much or too little. A high tax refund is nice to receive but it probably means that you've been paying too much. Instead, modify your W-4 and invest that extra money for a better return.

378 Draw up a will or estate plan. This document ensures that your assets are protected and divided according to your wishes, plus it will save you thousands of dollars in taxes. Use a lawyer to help you avoid any mistakes or complications.

379 Claim all the deductions you're allowed. Keep track of them throughout the year and stay informed of any tax law changes that could affect them.

380 Plan ahead. Developing a tax-planning strategy can save you a substantial amount of money.

381 Donate! If you itemize, your charitable contributions are fully deductible. Get written documentation for any donation over two hundred fifty dollars. You can also donate non-cash items like clothes, furniture and unused automobiles to charity and claim a deduction for the fair market value. Always ask for a receipt so you can deduct the items.

382 Avoid tax filing mistakes. Double-check everything, from your addition and subtraction to your Social Security number. Make sure your filing status and number of exemptions are correct. Be sure you sign your return. Eliminating these mistakes can keep you from costly penalties and fees.

What the Bible Says:

Dishonest money dwindles away, but he who gathers money little by little makes it grow.

PROVERBS 13:11

Cut Your Car Costs

Spending Less on Transportation

Staying within your transportation budget is just a matter of common sense. Tweaking a few of your driving habits can save you money on gas and maintenance and keep your car running longer. Here's what you can do.

Fuel Spending and Economy

383 Keep track of your gas mileage. This could alert you to maintenance issues before they become visible.

384 Increase your gas mileage by not resting your foot on the brake or clutch while you drive.

385 Purchase pre-paid gas cards. They're convenient, renewable and may offer discounts depending on the amount of gas you buy.

386 Walk or bike if you live in an urban area—at least for errands close to home. You'll save on gas and get exercise in the process.

387 Get the most out of your gas purchase. When the gas pump clicks off, get the extra half-cup of gas in the hose by lifting it higher than the handle while it's still in the tank.

388 Save time and gas by planning out your errands and getting them finished in one day instead of lots of little trips over several days.

389 Protect your gas mileage by driving with the windows up. Car-top carriers, bike racks and ski racks also create air drag for the car, thus reducing gas mileage. Use them only when you need to.

390 Pump gas yourself and avoid paying full-service prices.

391 Compare gasoline prices and avoid gas stations in higher traffic areas. They often charge more than stations just a few miles away.

392 Use the lowest grade of gasoline your owner's manual recommends. Most cars don't need premium gasoline.

393 Keep your tires properly inflated. Under-inflated tires can lower your fuel economy by up to two percent for every missing pound of pressure.

394 Make sure your engine is tuned. If it's not, it can use three percent to eight percent more gas.

395 Drive the speed limit. Going sixty-five miles per hour instead of the posted fifty-five lowers your gas mileage by about fifteen percent.

396 Shut off your car instead of letting the engine idle too long. You can waste between half a gallon and a gallon of gas per hour.

397 Accelerate slowly when starting from a stop and don't push the pedal all the way down. This ensures your carburetor will perform at peak efficiency.

398 Take road trips in the fall. Gas prices are generally cheaper during that time of year.

399 Consider purchasing a car with a manual transmission. They offer better fuel economy.

400 Make sure your trunk is empty. Extra weight can negatively affect your fuel economy.

401 Try not to "rev" your engine since this wastes fuel needlessly.

402 Buy gas early in the morning or later at night. Gas is densest during this time and you'll get more for your money since gas is measured by volume, not fuel concentration.

403 Fill your tank, but not all the way to the top. Overfilling will cause gas to spill out of the tank.

404 Drive steadily, avoiding jerky stops and starts, which waste fuel.

405 Accelerate before you reach a hill—not on it—to preserve gas mileage.

406 Stick to smooth, straight roads and avoid dirt or gravel roads. They can reduce your gas mileage by up to to thirty percent.

407 Remove snow and ice from your car during the winter. Any excess weight will bring down your gas mileage.

408 Use your cruise control, especially while driving on the highway. You'll improve your gas mileage if you keep your speed steady.

409 Consider radial tires. They provide great fuel economy and can cut your gas expenditures by two percent to three percent.

410 Use your air conditioner sparingly for better gas mileage. Your engine uses extra energy to power the air conditioner compressor.

Maintenance and Repair

411 Keep up on your car's routine maintenance. Regular oil changes, tire rotations, tune ups, etc., will ensure that your car runs better and longer, plus you'll get better gas mileage. Many mechanics offer coupons or discounts on these services.

412 Take care of small problems immediately. If you don't, they could turn into major and more expensive problems.

413 Brake earlier rather than later to avoid unnecessary wear and tear on your brakes.

414 Wipe windshield wipers with a mixture of vinegar and water before purchasing new ones. This will clean them and you may not have to replace them.

415 Purchase a small magnetic key safe to place under a bumper or somewhere else on your car. This comes in very handy if you get locked out and prevents an expensive locksmith fee.

416 Take an auto repair class and learn to perform routine maintenance yourself. The small investment in the class will definitely pay off.

417 Wash and wax your own car instead of paying to have it done. You'll save money and get the results you want.

418 Search out a knowledgeable and reputable mechanic who offers fair prices and communicates well about options and costs. Get referrals from friends and business associates.

Buying and Selling a Car

419 Look at purchasing a car from an auto auction or through your financial institution. Many banks have sales on vehicles that have been repossessed. This can be a great way to save on a used car.

420 Put off buying a new car until the one you already own gets too expensive to repair.

421 Bring any used car you're considering to a mechanic you trust before you buy. Don't get stuck with a lemon.

422 Be smart about buying a car. Know how much you can spend and what kind of car will best suit your needs. Research the model you're interested in, focusing on repair records, resale values, insurance costs and fuel efficiency. Get the car you can afford now and save for the one you want.

423 Shop around for the best loan. Determine how much you can borrow. Many financial experts suggest that transportation accounts for ten percent to fifteen percent of your monthly expenses. Make sure your loan doesn't penalize you for making pre-payments.

424 Know the right time to make a car purchase. The last two weeks of December are best because most people are Christmas shopping and dealers are looking for customers. July to October is another good time. Dealers are clearing out older cars to make room for the new model year during this time.

425 Research the costs and dealer incentives on the car you want to buy. You'll know how much the dealer paid for the car and can negotiate based on that information.

426 Do not pay cash for a deposit on a vehicle. If the deal doesn't go through, you can dispute a credit transaction but you may not get your cash back.

427 Avoid purchasing the extended warranty or credit life insurance when you buy a new car. Most of these are severely overpriced and are sources of high profits for dealerships.

428 Get educated before you ever consider leasing a vehicle. Leases can be very complicated and this makes it easy for sellers to hide extra costs.

429 Sell your car instead of trading it in to a dealer. You'll get a better deal.

430 Avoid "no-haggle" dealerships. You can save more by negotiating.

431 Always test drive a car before purchasing to make a more informed decision. A test drive can alert you to any potential problems with the engine, visibility, noise levels, etc.

432 Don't be upfront about the color of car you want. Otherwise, you may be told that the color you desire is in "short supply" and the price will suddenly go up.

433 Don't be afraid to walk away from the negotiations. The salesperson wants you to stay and may be willing to lower the price to keep you in your chair.

434 Bring your wife or husband with you when you go to purchase a car. He or she can act as someone who is not thoroughly convinced that this is the best deal you can get, which enhances your bargaining power.

Car Insurance

435 Compare prices. Utilize consumer information offered by your state's insurance division, then call around to several companies asking for quotes.

436 Look into getting a higher deductible, which leads to a lower premium.

437 Drop collision or comprehensive coverage on older cars. Determine how much your car is worth using the Kelly Blue Book or check with your bank. If it's less than one thousand dollars, you may end up paying more for coverage than you would be able to collect on a claim.

438 Look into insurance costs when you move. Rates are usually lower in rural areas and higher in cities.

439 Purchase a car with a good repair record and low theft rate. Insurance will generally be less expensive.

440 Ask your insurance agents about discounts. Most policies give discounts for safety features like air bags, antilock brakes and anti-theft devices, as well as many others.

441 Double check your insurance policy after you receive it and make sure you're getting the price you were quoted.

What the Bible Says:

Cast but a glance at riches, and they are gone, for they will surely sprout wings and fly off to the sky like an eagle.

PROVERBS 23:5

Smart Savings On The Basics

Keeping Your Utility Costs Down

We often take these services (and their fees) for granted, but it's surprisingly simple to lower your telephone, electric, gas and water bills. Start seeing these savings each month.

Telephone

442 Send an email, a card or write a letter instead of making a long distance phone call.

443 Use your cell phone if you have free minutes each month. Don't let them go to waste, but use them to make the calls you need.

444 Block 900# calls from your phone service.

445 When you make a long distance call, set a timer so you won't lose track of time and end up with a hefty bill.

446 Dial long distance calls directly. Avoid using the operator or directory assistance to connect you since these calls can be costly.

447 Cancel phone services you do not utilize often, like call waiting or three-way calling.

448 Use a phone book or Internet phone directories for free instead of paying for directory assistance.

449 Choose a long distance plan that allows you to call any day of the week. Many people have a hard time limiting their calls to specific days. If you can control your calling, track your phone and long distance usage and then research the plan that best fits your calling pattern.

450 Stay away from phone extras like *66 or *69. They often cost fifty cents or more each time you use them.

451 Purchase a calling card from a discount retailer. Many cards have rates as low as three or four cents per minute, and they are renewable. Be sure to read the fine print to ensure there are no hidden fees.

452 Consider switching services if a better rate is offered. When your provider calls to ask why you switched, ask if they can beat the rates you were given by the competition.

Cooling

453 Use fans to keep your home cool. They use about one-tenth as much electricity as an air conditioner and make it feel about ten degrees cooler. Use them in windows to bring in cooler air or to circulate cold air from the air conditioner through the house faster.

454 Turn the air conditioning up or off when you're out of the house. Buy an air conditioning timer if you would like to have your house cooled by the time you return home.

455 Test, clean and tune up your cooling system each year as the weather warms up. Clear outside vents of any leaves or debris that may have collected during the winter. Seal and insulate cooling system ducts in your house and make sure that furniture or drapes aren't blocking the flow of cool air.

456 Shade your cooling unit using small trees or shrubs—it will use up to ten percent less electricity than one in the sun.

457 Caulk around windows and doors. A one-eighth inch opening around two doorframes will let in as much warm air as a small window open six inches. Repair gaps and cracks in your foundation, on your roof or in windows to save on cooling costs.

458 Cool only the rooms necessary. Close doors or vents in rooms that are seldom used.

459 Turn off window air conditioners when you won't be using the room it's in for several hours.

460 Install white or neutrally colored blinds to keep the sun out.

461 Make sure your attic and crawl spaces are properly insulated.

462 Plant trees to shade your home and windows from the sun.

463 Turn off your furnace pilot light during the summer since it can contribute to additional heat in your house.

464 Use kitchen, bath and other exhaust fans sparingly to help keep cool air inside. Make sure windows and doors are shut tightly. Limit the number of trips in and out of your house on warm days.

465 Set your thermostat as high as you can within your comfort range. If your air conditioner is set at 78°F, it uses about forty percent less power than an air conditioner set at 72°F. Avoid placing TVs or lamps near a thermostat because of the heat they emanate.

466 Get an air conditioner that is the right size for your home. One that is too big or too small will not run efficiently.

467 Wear cool, loose-fitting clothes when the temperature is high to keep you cool and your air conditioning costs down.

468 Keep your hair shorter during the summer months if possible. This will help your body stay cooler.

469 Drink water and avoid sodas and alcoholic beverages on hot days.

Electricity

470 Dry heavier items like towels and blankets apart from your other laundry to reduce drying time and lower electricity costs. Include some netting or tulle when drying towels to allow more air to flow around and through them.

471 Check to see that any new appliances you purchase are energy efficient. This information can be found on the Energy Guide labels required by federal law.

472 Take advantage of the utility audits offered by many power companies. They can save you up to one hundred dollars per year.

473 Look into off-peak electric rates offered by your power company. The savings may compensate for the inconvenience.

474 Install timers on light switches that inadvertently get left on, like those found in closets, hallways, garages, bathrooms, etc.

475 Use fluorescent bulbs in lights that get used often. These bulbs last significantly longer and provide more light.

476 Install dimmer switches. They can reduce your electricity usage and extend your bulb life significantly.

477 Cook in your microwave instead of your oven. This can save you up to fifty percent in energy costs for cooking.

478 Add several clean towels to small laundry loads to decrease drying time.

479 Look into a dryer with a moisture sensor. This device turns off the dryer when the items inside are dry.

480 Keep refrigerators and freezers away from heat-producing appliances and out of direct sunlight. The added heat causes them to use more energy.

481 Defrost manual-defrost freezers regularly to save energy.

482 Clean stovetop burners and reflectors regularly. This will help them work more efficiently.

483 Turn off your burners a few minutes before the recommended cooking time if you have an electric stove. The burners will stay warm enough to finish the job and you'll save on electricity.

484 Clean your dishwasher filter regularly so it runs more efficiently.

485 Hang your clothes outside to dry. They'll smell great and you'll save on the cost to dry them.

Water

486 Purchase a tankless water heater. They last longer since there is no tank to rust and can save you nearly fifteen percent in standby energy losses.

487 Check the temperature on your water heater and make sure it is set between 115° and 120° Fahrenheit (46° to 50° Celsius). By lowering the temperature, you can save thirteen percent for each ten degrees Fahrenheit or five degrees Celsius lower.

488 Wash clothing in warm water and rinse in cold, which is much more energy efficient than the hot water cycle.

489 Use a soaker hose to water your lawn or garden instead of a sprinkler. This way you will water exactly where it's needed.

490 Start a compost pile instead of using the garbage disposal.

491 Water your lawn only when necessary and do it early in the morning or later in the evening when the water will not evaporate as quickly. Be sure you're watering the lawn or flowerbeds, not the sidewalk or driveway.

492 Do full loads of laundry. They typically use about twenty-one gallons of water, while a small load uses fourteen gallons. Several small loads will use much more water than two full loads.

493 Wash your dishes by hand instead of using the dishwasher. You use about nine gallons of water instead of the thirteen that your dishwasher uses.

494 Wait to run your dishwasher until you have a full load. Allow dishes to air-dry instead of using the heat cycle.

495 Store a pitcher of water in the refrigerator and drink from that instead of waiting for the faucet to cool.

496 Let unused ice cubes water your plants instead of melting in the sink.

497 Scrape dishes into the trash instead of into the sink under running water.

498 Pre-treat or pre-soak soiled clothing so you won't have to wash it twice.

499 Save on the cost of water and heating bills by installing a flow-restricting showerhead.

500 Add fabric softener to your washing machine at the appropriate time instead of at the end and running another rinse cycle. Set a timer while you do laundry so you know when to add it.

501 Don't use the toilet for a trash can. Avoid flushing items like cotton balls, dental floss and tissues.

502 Find ways to shorten your showers and avoid taking baths.

503 Turn off the tap water while brushing your teeth.

504 Install a gauge on sprinklers to prevent them from running if the ground is already saturated. This will help you cut down on the water bill.

505 Soak fruits and vegetables in a bowl of cool water instead of running water over them.

506 Make only the amount of coffee and tea that you will drink.

Heating

507 Use Venetian blinds to help keep energy costs down. In the winter they should be slanted, top to bottom, from indoors to outdoors to keep cool air behind the blinds.

508 Keep your thermostat set at 68° Fahrenheit during the day and lower it to 62° at night. Set it at 58° if you're away from home for more than four hours.

509 Reverse ceiling fans to push warm air downward.

510 Allow sunlight to warm your home. Keep blinds and drapes open during the day and closed at night. Make certain south-facing windows are clean and screens removed. These steps can increase solar warmth by forty percent.

511 Make sure your house is properly insulated and any holes or gaps repaired. Use weather stripping or caulking around door and window frames.

512 Install storm or thermal windows in your home. The air that gets trapped between the two panes acts as a thermal insulator and keeps heated air inside.

513 Keep registers clear and clean.

514 Look into purchasing a heat pump. They are the most efficient form of electric heating for homes in moderate climates and can shave twenty-five to seventy-five percent from your heating bill compared to a conventional air-source pump. Repairs can be costly, however, because the units are located underground.

515 Keep your furnace clean, lubricated and properly adjusted. Replace your filter often. Replace an older furnace with a new, energy-efficient model.

516 Keep your fireplace damper closed when not in use. Purchase C-shaped grates or a heat-exchange system to circulate the heat throughout your home when you do use your fireplace. Caulk leaks around your fireplace.

517 Close doors and vents to rooms that are not in use.

518 Insulate your home using furniture and wall hangings. Use filled bookcases, area rugs and fabric wall hangings on outside non-mass walls. Cover walls with carpet and padding to reduce heat transfer. Place overstuffed furniture in northern rooms and furniture with skirts in areas with drafts.

Appliances

519 Keep your refrigerator and freezer at the recommended temperatures: 38° to 40° Fahrenheit for the refrigerator and 5° Fahrenheit for the freezer. Keep freezers used for long-term food storage set at 0° to -5° Fahrenheit.

520 Keep your refrigerator full. (Fill it with bowls of water if you don't have a lot of food stored in it.) This allows it to retain cold better.

521 Check the seal on your refrigerator door by closing it over a piece of paper or dollar bill. If you can pull it out easily, the seal may need to be replaced.

522 Keep appliances lint- and dust-free. Dryer lint can impede airflow, making drying times longer. Dusty refrigerator condenser coils can make the unit less energy efficient.

523 Open your oven only when necessary while you're baking. The temperature is lowered by 25° each time you open the oven door.

524 Bake several dishes at one time to save both energy and time.

525 Look into purchasing new appliances if the ones you own are over ten years old. Newer models use thirty percent less electricity.

What the Bible Says:

Wealth and honor come from you; you are the ruler of all things. In your hands are strength and power to exalt and give strength to all.

1 CHRONICLES 29:12

Avoiding The Tourist Trap
Take a Vacation for Less

A vacation allows you to escape from the pressures of work, school and other daily activities, but don't let it put added stress on your pocketbook. Enjoy your time away without worrying about your budget with these helpful suggestions.

Before You Go

526 Purchase snacks, drinks and other goodies before you leave to avoid fast food drive-thrus or convenience stores.

527 Get several of your meals at a grocery store while you're on vacation. You can purchase complete meals at the deli counter for less than you would pay in a restaurant, or put together your own meal of bread or crackers along with cheese, salami, fresh fruits and vegetables and drinks.

528 Make activity bags for your kids with books, paper, pens, games, puzzles and maps to trace your route.

On the Way

529 Spend the nights in KOA cabins while you travel. They are clean and have nice restrooms. If you decide to go this route, be sure to pack breakfast food. Be adventurous and cook breakfast over a campfire.

530 Take bathroom breaks at rest stops instead of gas stations, where you could be tempted by the snacks and sodas for sale.

531 Stay in smaller towns, away from tourist attractions, if camping doesn't appeal to you. Hotel and restaurant prices are lower the farther away you stay from tourist attractions.

532 Call the specific location when you are staying at a chain hotel or motel. You can often get a lower rate by doing that instead of calling the chain's 800 number.

533 Don't get caught in tourist traps while shopping on vacation. Shop where the local residents do.

534 Always ask if the hotel or motel has a better rate to offer you. They often do.

Saving on Flights

535 Book your flight early. It's much cheaper to plan ahead than to make reservations at the last minute.

536 Make your travel plans flexible. It's less expensive to stay over on a Saturday night, travel a few hours earlier or fly to a city near your final destination and drive the rest of the way.

537 Fly out of airports that offer cheaper fares. Even if you have drive a little farther, you'll end up saving money on a round-trip ticket.

538 Avoid travel on Friday evening or Monday morning, which are the busiest times. Airlines often charge extra.

539 Fly during off-peak times and avoid holidays. You'll get a lower airfare and avoid massive crowds.

540 Travel between November 1 and December 15, the slowest season for travel. (Thanksgiving weekend is the exception during this time.) This is a great time for low rates on overseas flights.

541 Ask for the lowest rate possible when you make your reservation.

542 Take advantage of frequent flier programs to help offset the cost of travel.

543 Purchase your airline tickets on weekdays, not weekends. Prices tend to go up on weekends and back down on weekdays.

544 Take advantage of bereavement fares when you must travel because of the death of a loved one. You usually do not have to pay full price if flying under these circumstances.

545 Ask for discounts on children's airfare. Many airlines offer lower prices if you ask.

Renting a Car

546 Rent a vehicle at an agency away from the airport. You will often pay less than if you rent a car at the airport.

547 Shop around for the best rate when renting a car. Be sure to ask about additional charges and special offers.

548 Look into membership rate discounts whenever you rent a vehicle.

549 Watch car rental insurance and check with your insurance agent in advance to avoid duplicating any coverage you may already have.

General

550 Take day trips or long weekend trips. These are inexpensive ways to take a break from the hectic pace of work and other activities.

551 Enjoy a stay-at-home vacation and catch up on things you haven't had the time to do.

552 Stay with relatives while on vacation. It's a great way to save on food and lodging, plus you have your own personal tour guides to attractions in the area.

553 Take up camping. It's cheaper than staying at a hotel or motel and is a vacation in and of itself.

554 Travel by train. Train fares can be cheaper than plane tickets for cross-country travel, plus it's a relaxing way to see the country.

555 Pack wisely when you travel. Purchasing sundries like shampoo and razors from hotels or tourist shops can get expensive.

556 Take your vacation in Washington, D.C. Most of its tourist sites do not charge admission. Take advantage of tours you can get through your senators or representatives.

557 Stay in business-oriented hotels on weekends. They will often give you a discount during this time because their occupancy rates plummet on weekends.

558 Ask for a long-term rate if you will be staying five consecutive nights. You may be able to receive a discount.

559 Travel in the off-season. You can save on cruises, amusement park admission, resort prices, etc.

560 Use a special skill or talent to cruise for free. Many cruises need people to lead games, activities, give lectures or provide daycare.

561 Tell the cruise line if you are traveling to celebrate a special occasion like a marriage or anniversary. They will often offer you a discount off of the standard fare.

562 Pack your clothes carefully and logically to avoid expensive hotel cleaning bills. Put bulky items like jeans and sweaters at the bottom of your suitcase. Pack easily wrinkled items in plastic. Use plastic bags to pack items like shampoo and soaps to avoid messy spills.

What the Bible Says:

But seek first his kingdom and his righteousness, and all these things will be given to you as well.

MATTHEW 6:33

Here Comes The Bride

Budget-Minded Weddings

A beautiful wedding is every couple's dream. Yet with the average American wedding costing over nineteen thousand dollars, it's easy to go overboard and spend a bundle. Here are some ideas for making a memorable wedding day without breaking the bank.

563 Keep the proper perspective. A wedding is a once-in-a-lifetime event, but it shouldn't take a lifetime to pay for it. Avoid comparisons with friends or relatives. Begin by looking at the big picture: Would you rather spend five thousand dollars on a dress or perhaps apply this to a down payment on a house? Set priorities and a budget and stick to them.

564 Plan your wedding date for off-peak times. You can get better deals on virtually every wedding service if you schedule your wedding in one of the "off-season" months. Your best bets are early November (before the holiday rush), January, February (avoid Valentine's Day, when flower prices peak), or March. And hold your wedding on a day other than Saturday—the most popular and expensive day to rent reception areas.

565 Shop around for the right wedding dress. An off-the-rack wedding dress (yes, they do exist) can cost less than two hundred dollars. Or use the philosophy that grooms and ushers follow: Rent the dress. Other options for low-cost dresses include wedding outlets, second-hand shops, newspaper ads, consignment shops and the Internet. Save an additional two hundred dollars by making your own veil for twenty dollars. Many craft stores sell supplies and books to show you how.

566 Keep your reception small and simple. Invite anyone to the wedding but limit the reception size since your single biggest cost will be reception food and alcohol. Choose less-expensive entrees, such as chicken or pasta instead of beef or seafood. Limit alcohol choices to beer and wine bought in bulk or just serve coffee, tea and soft drinks. Better yet, change the time of your reception. A late-morning brunch costs less per plate than dinner, and there should be far less alcohol poured earlier in the day.

567 Decorate strategically. Silk arrangements are cheaper than fresh flowers, plus they can be rented. Interweave the bouquets with accents of fresh, in-season flowers grown locally. Consider candles or tiny white lights to add drama and style with little cost. An outdoor location, historical building or spectacular cathedral can provide natural beauty without embellishment.

568 Skip the band. Music for your reception can be provided inexpensively with some favorite CDs and a multi-disc system. If your reception includes dancing, a disc jockey will usually provide greater selection and lower expense than a band. For a formal affair, replace the expensive wedding orchestra with a chamber music trio from a music school.

569 Use professional photographers as needed. A professional photographer or video crew can run thousands of dollars—so bid out the process. Hire the photographer for a limited time slot such as some post-ceremony formal photos or early reception pictures. Check out local universities for qualified and inexpensive videographers or have an experienced friend videotape the event. Place disposable cameras on each table for guests to take candid shots.

What the Bible Says:

Trust in the Lord with all of your heart and lean not on your own understanding; in all your ways acknowledge him, and he will make your paths straight.

PROVERBS 3:5-6

Free Is Fabulous!

The best way to save money is to get something for nothing (or at least next to nothing). Here's a list of resources and organizations that offer free or low cost products and services. Check them out!

Note: Many of the items listed in this section are available only on the Internet. If you don't have Internet access available, go to your local library and use it for free. These websites and links were valid at press time but are subject to change due to the fluid nature of the Internet. And as always, use good judgment whenever downloading something from the Internet.

570 Go to www.refundsweepers.com for a great list of links to free samples from major corporations.

571 You can vacation absolutely free by enlisting six or more paying passengers to form a tour group in a foreign country. Ask a reputable travel agency how.

572 Babies Online helps parents show off their new babies to friends and family around the world with their automated birth announcement system! Your baby gets his or her own web page, complete with pictures, and it's free. Check it out at www.babies-online.com

573 Claim your FREE subscription to *BabyTalk* magazine, America's number one guide to birth and your baby's first year of life. Simply fill out the form at www.babiesonline.com/babytalk/

574 Tons of family-friendly FREEBIES online at My Freebies. (www.myfreebies.com) Frugal shoppers will also find great coupon offers and programs too!

575 If your little one just started potty training, or will start soon, help him along with a set of FREE potty training materials (including the Charmin Roll Ruler). www.charmin.com

576 Using Homestead (www.homestead.com), GeoCities (www.geocities.com) and Tripod (www.tripod.com), you can build a free website and have it hosted for free, too. Homestead is targeted more to home users than business people, but shopping tools are also available. You can, for instance, add a shopping cart to your site and even accept credit card payments. And it's straightforward. You can start with one of the supplied templates and customize it for your purposes by dragging and dropping elements right onto the page. Among other things, you can add graphics, sound and video; provide chat and polling services; and offer local weather forecasts.

577 Many manufacturers offer starter kits for parents of multiple births (twin-quad). Just call and ask:

- Beechnut Food Corporation: 800-523-6633
- Evenflo Products: 800-356-BABY
- Gerber: 800-4-GERBER
- Johnson and Johnson: 800-526-3967
- Kimberly Clark (Huggies diapers): 800-544-1847
- Mead and Johnson (Enfamil Baby Formula): 800-222-9123
- Playtex: 800-222-0543
- Procter and Gamble (Pampers and Luvs diapers): Parents of triplets or more can call 800-543-0480
- The First Years: 800-533-6708

578 Get your baby's first pair of shoes FREE! Bring your baby with you to Payless® fill out a registration card, and get your baby's shoes free.

579 The President and First Lady of the United States will gladly send you a congratulations card for your new baby. Add a very special keepsake to your baby book! Send your request along with your baby's name, address and birth date to: White House Greetings Office, Room 39, Washington D.C. 20500.

580 Track your family tree online FREE. The world's leading genealogy site offers a comprehensive search of more than one billion names, free software for you to download and the capability to record generations of history right on your computer. www.ancestry.com

581 Receive complimentary samples from your favorite brands. From nutrition bars to sunless tanning lotion, here you can try it all. Become a member—it's free. www.StartSampling.com

582 FREE desktop screensaver: Put your personal photos into the program, or mail your friends and family personalized e-postcards. www.webshots.com

FREEBIES

583 FREE software! Choose from a tremendous selection of titles—sports, hobbies and games, health and more. Available at www.valpak.com /member/kestral_nonmember_content.jsp.

584 Break-Thru Safety Tassles offers FREE cleats or break-away safety tassels to help get started baby-proofing your home. (More than 140 children have died in the United States since 1981 by strangulation from window treatment cords.) Go to www.nobrainerblinds.com/info/child.asp.

585 The Motley Fool will help you begin your journey to financial independence. Receive the FREE "13 Steps to Investing Foolishly" guide and other nifty investment freebies when you register! Visit www.fool.com.

586 FREE McGruff comic book from McGruff.org, a site devoted to the cartoon crime dog who teaches kids how to be safe and healthy. Go to www.mcgruff.org/order.htm.

587 Reviews, ratings and descriptions of the Internet's top FREEWARE games are available in this game directory. Categories include card games, arcade, action, strategy, board games and adventure and simulation titles. Games include downloadable Windows titles, as well as Java and Shockwave games. See www.free-games.to.

588 Get the next issue of *Home Business Connection* magazine totally FREE. It has over 229 money-makers that you can do from home, plus free offers and samples. Visit www.freemoneymaking-magazine.com

589 Here's a roundup of FREE educational, fun games for children from Microsoft. Titles include *The Magic Schoolbus, Escaping Monkey, Skeleton Puzzle* and *Meteor Meltdown*. It's found at www.microsoft.com/kids/freestuff/.

590 Have all the best coupons and FREEBIES emailed to you weekly. Go to www.directcoupons.com.

591 Tired of stale, delayed stock quotes? This FREE service gives you real-time quotes that you can retrieve as fast as your Internet connection will allow. See www.FreeRealTime.com

592 Receive an American flag decal FREE. This is a static-cling decal that adheres to any surface. Visit www.freeamericanflags.com

593 Receive a FREE U.S. flag magnet, plus look into other free offers like sweepstakes and surveys. Go to www.free-flags.com.

594 Your choice of either Essential Protein or Essential IsoFlavones from www.mothersoy.com, sellers of soy protein concentrate products.

595 Your choice of either Oil of Olay Total Effects Moisturizer UV Fomula or Total Effects Hand and Body Treatment FREE. These moisturizer products claim "age-defying benefits." Go to www.total-effects.com/sample/sample.shtml.

596 Click the "Coupons and FREE STUFF" link near the top of the page at www.lampsplus.com and request a coupon, good for a free light bulb, which you may redeem at any location of Lamps Plus, which has retail stores in thirty-eight states.

597 Looking for coupons on the Web? This directory offers a roundup of coupons for restaurants, merchants, food and more. Visit www.big-coupons.com.

598 Look into FREE samples, contests, catalogs, gift certificates, freeware, opportunities for earning cash and more. See www.free2try.com.

599 Get a free Hot Wheels car for your child's birthday. Log on to www.hotwheels.com/2001 /birthdayclub/index.asp to find out how.

600 Create delicious new recipes with the free cook-book you can get from Swanson. Sign up for it at www.swansonbroth.com/cookbook_offer.asp.

Resource Guide

Looking for information to help you manage and save your money? Here's a list of resources that offer suggestions and guidance from a Christian perspective.

- *Money, Possessions and Eternity* by Randy Alcorn

- *The Treasure Principle* by Randy Alcorn

- *A Woman's Guide to Financial Peace of Mind* by Ron and Judy Blue

- *Generous Living* by Ron Blue

- *Master Your Money* by Ron Blue

- *Taming the Money Monster* by Ron Blue

- *How to Manage Your Money* by Larry Burkett

- *Money in Marriage* by Larry Burkett

- *Money Management for College Students* by Larry Burkett

- *Money Matters—Radio Host Answers All Your Questions* by Larry Burkett

- *Your Finances in Changing Times* by Larry Burkett

- *Absolutely Amazing Ways to Save Money on Everything* by James L. Paris

- *Sound Mind Investing* by Austin Pryor

940535

Cannot be combined with other coupons or Perks Shopping Sprees. Not to be used toward the purchase of gift certificates, VBS, electronics, church and home school curriculum or church supplies. No price adjustments on merchandise previously purchased. Available in stores on in-stock items only—not applicable on internet or phone orders.

940537

Cannot be combined with other coupons or Perks Shopping Sprees. Not to be used toward the purchase of gift certificates, VBS, electronics, church and home school curriculum or church supplies. No price adjustments on merchandise previously purchased. Available in stores on in-stock items only—not applicable on internet or phone orders.

940538

Cannot be combined with other coupons or Perks Shopping Sprees. Not to be used toward the purchase of gift certificates, VBS, electronics, church and home school curriculum or church supplies. No price adjustments on merchandise previously purchased. Available in stores on in-stock items only—not applicable on internet or phone orders.

940539

Cannot be combined with other coupons or Perks Shopping Sprees. Not to be used toward the purchase of gift certificates, VBS, electronics, church and home school curriculum or church supplies. No price adjustments on merchandise previously purchased. Available in stores on in-stock items only—not applicable on internet or phone orders.

FAMILY
CHRISTIAN STORES

940540

Cannot be combined with other coupons or Perks Shopping Sprees. Not to be used toward the purchase of gift certificates, VBS, electronics, church and home school curriculum or church supplies. No price adjustments on merchandise previously purchased. Available in stores on in-stock items only–not applicable on internet or phone orders.

FAMILY
CHRISTIAN STORES

940542

Cannot be combined with other coupons or Perks Shopping Sprees. Not to be used toward the purchase of gift certificates, VBS, electronics, church and home school curriculum or church supplies. No price adjustments on merchandise previously purchased. Available in stores on in-stock items only–not applicable on internet or phone orders.

FAMILY
CHRISTIAN STORES

940543

nnot be combined with other coupons or Perks Shopping Sprees. Not to be used toward
 purchase of gift certificates, VBS, electronics, church and home school curriculum or
ch supplies. No price adjustments on merchandise previously purchased. Available in stores on in-stock items only–not applicable on internet or phone orders.

FAMILY
CHRISTIAN STORES

940544

Cannot be combined with other coupons or Perks Shopping Sprees. Not to be used toward the purchase of gift certificates, VBS, electronics, church and home school curriculum or church supplies. No price adjustments on merchandise previously purchased. Available in stores on in-stock items only–not applicable on internet or phone orders.

FamiLY
CHRISTIAN STORES

940545

Cannot be combined with other coupons or Perks Shopping Sprees. Not to be used toward the purchase of gift certificates, VBS, electronics, church and home school curriculum or church supplies. No price adjustments on merchandise previously purchased. Available in stores on in-stock items only–not applicable on internet or phone orders.

FamiLY
CHRISTIAN STORES

940546

Cannot be combined with other coupons or Perks Shopping Sprees. Not to be used toward the purchase of gift certificates, VBS, electronics, church and home school curriculum or church supplies. No price adjustments on merchandise previously purchased. Available in stores on in-stock items only–not applicable on internet or phone orders.

FamiLY
CHRISTIAN STORES

940547

Cannot be combined with other coupons or Perks Shopping Sprees. Not to be used toward the purchase of gift certificates, VBS, electronics, church and home school curriculum or church supplies. No price adjustments on merchandise previously purchased. Available in stores on in-stock items only–not applicable on internet or phone orders.

FamiLY
CHRISTIAN STORES

940548

Cannot be combined with other coupons or Perks Shopping Sprees. Not to be used toward the purchase of gift certificates, VBS, electronics, church and home school curriculum or church supplies. No price adjustments on merchandise previously purchased. Available in stores on in-stock items only–not applicable on internet or phone orders.

ACTION STEPS

_____

_____

_____

_____

_____

_____

_____

_____

_____

_____

_____

_____

_____

_____

_____

_____

ACTION STEPS

_____

_____

_____

_____

_____

_____

_____

_____

_____

_____

_____

_____

_____

_____

_____

_____

_____

ACTION STEPS

_____

_____

_____

_____

_____

_____

_____

_____

_____

_____

_____

_____

_____

_____

_____

_____

ACTION STEPS

_____

_____

_____

_____

_____

_____

_____

_____

_____

_____

_____

_____

_____

_____

_____

_____

ACTION STEPS

_____

_____

_____

_____

_____

_____

_____

_____

_____

_____

_____

_____

_____

_____

_____

_____

_____

ACTION STEPS

_____

_____

_____

_____

_____

_____

_____

_____

_____

_____

_____

_____

_____

_____

_____

_____

_____

ACTION STEPS

_____

_____

_____

_____

_____

_____

_____

_____

_____

_____

_____

_____

_____

_____

_____

_____

_____

ACTION STEPS

_____

_____

_____

_____

_____

_____

_____

_____

_____

_____

_____

_____

_____

_____

_____

_____

_____

_____